PAST & PRESENT

OREGON CITY

OPPOSITE: Oregon City's Young Men's Christian Association (YMCA), initially organized in 1876, met with renewed interest in 1896 and gathered in local halls and churches until the completion of their three-story facility at 1023–1025 Main Street in 1899. However, interest again waned by this 1905 photograph, and the building was sold and later converted into a hay and grain store and warehouse. A parking lot replaced the structure in the 1960s, and a county building filled the site the following decade. (Courtesy Clackamas County Historical Society.)

OREGON CITY

Johna Sans Heintz and Jo Lynn Dow

To the early photographers and authors whose pictorial and penned accounts chronicled Oregon City's growth, evolution, and spirit and whose paths we were fortunate to retrace.

Library of Congress Control Number: 2023943282

Published by Arcadia Publishing
Charleston, South Carolina

Printed in the United States of America

For all general information, please contact Arcadia Publishing:
Telephone 843-853-2070
Fax 843-853-0044
E-mail sales@arcadiapublishing.com

Visit us on the Internet at www.arcadiapublishing.com

ON THE FRONT COVER: The intersection at Main and Seventh Streets emerged as Oregon City's crossroads in 1888, following the construction of the suspension bridge. Initially quartered by simple structures, the junction evolved into a commercial center where one accessed transportation, merchants, restaurants, legal and financial services, and the popular popcorn vendor. Renowned photographer Ralph Eddy immortalized Oregon City's vitality in about 1925 while capturing the pedestrian's perspective upon entering the city's bustling core from the Arch Bridge approach. (Courtesy Clackamas County Historical Society.)

ON THE BACK COVER: As Oregon City evolved, iconic images, such as this c. 1893 photograph, captured transformations that defined the city's distinctive townscape—unmatched by any American city. Geological formations offered a backdrop to architectural growth and provided a vertical foundation, scaled by pre-elevator staircases, that directed upper-level expansion. This photograph encapsulated Oregon City when steamboats ran the river, William Singer's abandoned mill divided the bluff over Eighth Street, and the Chase mansion overlooked the city. (Courtesy Clackamas County Historical Society.)

CONTENTS

Acknowledgments   vii
Introduction   ix

1.   In the Spray of the Falls   11

2.   Beyond the Bend and the Bridge   29

3.   Onto the Heights   43

4.   Roads, River, and Rail   69

5.   A Sense of Community   83

ACKNOWLEDGMENTS

This work was only possible because the following individuals, organizations, and fellow history enthusiasts graciously and willingly offered their assistance.

First, we want to thank the Clackamas County Historical Society (CCHS) for generously permitting us to share historical images from their remarkable photo collection.

Next, words cannot express how grateful and indebted we are to Steve Bennett. Steve spent numerous hours following our scribbled notes and hurried emails, researching city records, and joining us down branching rabbit holes. Steve was profoundly invaluable to the production of this book.

We also extend our gratitude to Waldo McGinnis, who always patiently and generously stretched his time and shared his talent when needed.

We are ever grateful to Mayor Denyse McGriff, Jim Nicita, Confederated Tribes of Grand Ronde Historian Dakota Zimmer, and Julie Blumel, who, despite their busy schedule, kindly found time to read our draft.

We deeply thank Sandy McGuire, Doug and Stella Shannon, and Steve Dietz for their knowledge, research, and nostalgic recollections. We express our heartfelt gratitude to Michelle Gaynor, whose adventurous spirit, ladder duty, and traffic watch were instrumental in helping capture challenging vantage points. We want to extend our deepest appreciation to Sandy King, Rose Kutch, and Adrian Wegner, who willingly rushed to our aid.

We are incredibly grateful to the Oregon City Fire Department for going further than we could have dreamed by orchestrating, staging, and reproducing the "now" version of the "then" photograph. We extend a huge thank you to Cyrus Facchini and Connie Jarrett for standing in for our "now" image to share alongside the "then" version. We further extend our appreciation to Dora Mills (Elks Lodge), Kaleb Coleus (The Highland Stillhouse), and Candice Henkin (Oregon City School District) for so kindly providing historical or updated information.

We express our sincere gratitude to the Oregon State Archives, Old Oregon Photos, and the Willamette Falls and Landings Heritage Area Coalition (WFLHAC), who continue to preserve historical photographs and who graciously allowed us to share their beautiful images. We thank past amateur and professional photographers whose skillful eyes captured and preserved history. Lastly, our heartfelt gratitude goes to dear friends and family, who are too many to list. We were profoundly motivated by their support, interest, enthusiasm, patience, and encouragement over the past two years.

Unless otherwise noted, all historical images are from CCHS's historical photograph collection. Photographer and coauthor Jo Lynn Dow captured all present images.

INTRODUCTION

Oregon City, situated on the east bank of the Willamette River, a landscape shaped by volcanic flow and carved by floods, sits perched amidst a backdrop of exposed basalt cliffs and the Willamette Falls. The region, the ancestral homelands of regional tribes, has hosted continuous settlements—communities that dwelled, traded, and fished along the river's shores—since time immemorial.

By the 1840s and the influx of immigrants, the Falls region emerged as an industrial core, luring Euro-American opportunists and re-settlers to travel west into Oregon Country, the new Eden, the land of opportunity, and Oregon City. However, what welcomed some ostracized others. The government and provisional regulations targeted non-Europeans and non-citizens, ensuring their removal, exclusion, and expulsion through treaties, voting, and laws.

Oregon City, the first incorporated US city west of the Rocky Mountains and the first capital of the Oregon Territory, would, by reason, become distinctive through additional "firsts" that directed religion, industry, and technology. Over the decades, these enterprises drew an industrial workforce and entrepreneurial ventures, propelling development, pushing merchants and tradespeople north, and forcing the townscape to conform to growth. As a result, dwellings bracketed by the river, the basalt wall, and flourishing mills increasingly moved to the bluff—more readily after cliffside staircases supplemented the steep climb. By 1915, pedestrians accessed the city's levels using an outdoor lift, the only municipal elevator in the country.

Many of Oregon City's landmarks benefitted from the Works Progress Administration (WPA) during the Great Depression in the 1930s. The WPA, under the Second New Deal program, offered employment and, through grants and labor, provided public works projects that renovated, constructed, and rebuilt structures such as the Barclay House, the Barclay School, the 1935 municipal swimming pool, the 1936 redbrick Clackamas County Courthouse, the McLoughlin Promenade, the Grand Staircase, Singer Hill Creek Falls, McLoughlin Boulevard, and the restoration and preservation of the McLoughlin House.

Oregon City's unique characteristics, landmarks, and history—the "firsts"—set the city apart. However, these features would only exist because an individual or a collective group offered ideas, suggested change, and formed collaborations, perpetuating the city's development. The stories told in the following pages are theirs. We use their words where possible, for their experience humanizes what would, to some, become mundane dates and places. Their comments, observations, and reporting were curated from local newspapers printed before time had yet to manipulate perspective, cloud realities, and ultimately lose the names of those whose footsteps we trace.

Finally, though the ensuing pages reflect the city's evolution from then to now, the imagery in the following excerpt evokes an enduring familiarity despite its appearance in the 1869 publication.

"Besides having a rocky foundation, Oregon City has a rocky wall extending nearly its whole length, a distance of about half a mile. This wall is about one hundred feet in height, and it separates the *lower* from the *upper* town. The lower town is built on a narrow plateau, bounded by the wall on the one side and the river on the other. The city is principally composed of a double row of houses on each side of one street running through the middle of the plateau. This plateau at its northern extremity opens into a river bottom about half a mile in width and a mile in length. This river bottom is looked upon by the surrounding houses rather suspiciously; instead of boldly entering upon and taking possession of it, they stand aloof on lofty eminences and eye it with a dubious aspect. The reason of this is that this beautiful and rich river bottom oftentimes and without notice, becomes the bottom of the river. The upper town, which is composed principally of dwelling houses, has an area of half a mile in width and three-fourths of a mile in length. This part of town has a healthy location and is very picturesque in appearance. The city contains about one thousand inhabitants, five churches, two grist mills, a paper mill, a foundry and a woolen factory. This factory has about seventeen hundred spindles and is in full operation. The principal feature in Oregon City is its unrivaled water power; indeed the whole of the Wallamet river might be used, if necessary, for this purpose. Oregon City is no doubt destined to become the chief manufacturing city of Oregon and perhaps of the whole Pacific Coast."

—*The Weekly Enterprise*
Oregon City, Oregon
April 17, 1869

IN THE SPRAY OF THE FALLS

The tower view from Oregon City's new Second Empire courthouse, in 1885, provided a spectacular 360-degree panorama of the growing city and beyond. The view, one not observable from the bluff, followed Main Street south, over the Barclay house rooftop, through the Seventh Street intersection, and looked directly into the mills.

Bill Green was honored in 1955 as the first letter carrier to deliver mail via the new municipal elevator. During the inaugural route, Green paused inside the elevator's observation deck to overlook the city's post office at Fifth and Main Streets, where he later served as postmaster. Across the river, the expansive West Linn paper mill contrasted Main Street's seemingly diminutive architecture, foreshadowing its imminent industry-driven demolition. Past elevator operator Cyrus Facchini observed the modern landscape nearly 70 years later.

The c. 1873 upriver view from Fourth Street depicts Oregon City's evolution from the sparsely populated mill town illustrated by 1840s–1850s artists Paul Kane, Capt. Henry Warre, and John Mix Stanley into an emerging industrial center positioned to drive city growth. Their works portrayed members of local Indigenous populations, soon forcibly removed under government treaties. In 2019, the Confederated Tribes of Grand Ronde, descendants of those depicted in the paintings, purchased the shuttered mill site, renamed Tumwata Village, for restoration.

By 1894, as Oregon City's mills flourished, neighboring proprietors capitalized on the industrial workforce and offered lodgings, saloons, and general goods and services. Increasingly, however, the manufacturing core expanded, driving merchants and residents north. Finally, though growth stabilized at Fifth Street, the enterprises that laid the city's early foundation simultaneously led to its decimation. (Past, courtesy Old Oregon Photos and WFLHAC.)

IN THE SPRAY OF THE FALLS

The Charman & Company Drug Store moved into their new brick building at 409 Main Street in 1890. They were joined the following year by the Livermore Hotel, renamed the Electric Hotel when new proprietors took ownership. The electrically illuminated lodgings, photographed in 1895, offered first-class accommodations and front-door access to the electric Eastside Railway, which shuttled commuters to and from Portland. A parking lot replaced the structure around 1960. Today, the cleared land patiently awaits a brighter future.

Following the Arch Bridge construction in 1922, the city planned to continue Pacific Highway bridge traffic down Seventh Street to Railroad Avenue, then south. However, opponents suggested a Main to Fifth Street route instead, citing the alternative required $50,000 in structural demolition. Ultimately, the Fifth Street passage prevailed. However, despite earlier arguments against demolition, these structures lining Fifth Street in about 1929 were razed to accommodate McLoughlin Boulevard in the 1930s. (Past, courtesy Oregon State Archives, Oregon Department of Transportation, OHDG797.)

IN THE SPRAY OF THE FALLS

"For all kinds of furniture that is not a bit wore, just call on Mr. G.H. Young of the Secondhand store." George Young (center right), photographed in 1910 with unidentified colleagues, briefly traded from 505 Main Street before relocating one doorway north. The Chicago Store, an apparel retailer, occupied the space until 1913, when a fire, blazing with "diabolical energy," decimated the structure. The current building, constructed shortly after, has housed a pool hall, cigar store, and taverns.

By 1892, the single-story building, contracted by the Latourettes, Davids, and Barlows, occupied 502–510 Main Street. The new structure adjoined the Latourettes' existing Commercial Bank building and replaced a blacksmith's shop and an undertaking parlor, formerly Amory Holbrook's law office. After the bank's 1961 demolition, a support pilaster, a remnant of the bank's stone facade, remained at the structure's northwest corner. West Linn school students, photographed in 1931, toured the telephone company and likely the post office, both neighboring tenants.

In 1894, the Fountain Hose Company trained among spectators outside 516–520 Main Street, where three years before, a fire had destroyed the earlier buildings. After reconstruction, Wilson and Cooke returned to their stand, and Bellomy & Busch leased the neighboring shop. The buildings survived until 1937, when the Safeway Corporation built a store in their place. The structure's current designation as the "Territorial Building" acknowledges Oregon's first territorial statehouse, once located at the northwest corner of the adjacent parking lot.

Before the superhighway routed US Route 99E to Fifth Street along the river's edge in the 1930s, the Pacific Highway passed directly down Oregon City's Main Street. This stretch, photographed south of Sixth Street around 1939, remained notably accommodating, providing motorists with overnight lodgings, meals, and automobile services. However, after the completion of Interstate 5 in the 1960s and, later, the George Abernethy Bridge along Interstate 205 in 1970, the popularity of the Oregon City routes declined.

IN THE SPRAY OF THE FALLS

The Myers Building, at 603 Main Street, maintains distinction as Oregon City's oldest commercial building. The 1860s corner structure, small and defined in this 1910 photograph, was integrated into a two-story building in the 1870s and housed the Bank of Oregon City and, in 1872, hosted the Chinese Free Masons. Across Main Street, the modern Stevens Building replaced the wood frame structure in 1929. Looking north, the horse-drawn buggy and electric streetcar marked the junction between time-honored transportation and modern technology.

In 1929, property investor Mertie Stevens replaced the 1890 wood frame structure at 610 Main Street with a larger brick commercial block. The new building dominated the wedge-shaped lot, extending east toward Railroad Avenue. The additional space accommodated multiple tenants, including JCPenney, Bill West's Fountain and Smoke Shop, a barber and beauty shop, and a jeweler. In 1950, a fire gutted the building, and subsequent restoration modernized the brick facade. Later renovations concealed the remaining brick with layers of stucco.

On June 26, 1896, the *Oregon City Enterprise,* advantaged with a bird's-eye view over Main Street, reported the arrival of the Bank of Oregon City's new spherical Corliss safe. The device, marketed as burglar-proof, arrived on a wagon bed "drawn by four powerful horses."

Upon its arrival, curious onlookers gathered in front of the Myers Building at 603 Main Street to welcome the "mysterious article." Today, the "mechanical curiosity" is displayed in the foyer of Oregon City's KeyBank building.

The Classic Revival–style Elks Lodge, constructed in 1912, overlooked the Willamette River at 610 Water Street, where Francis Ermatinger's home originally stood. However, the grand structure, photographed in 1914, was lost when a fire destroyed the building in 1922. A new Mission Revival–style Elks Lodge was constructed in a Mission Revival style the following year and purposefully included reinforced fire-resistant concrete walls. Considerable renovations and expansions in 1949 and 1968 completely enveloped the 1923 structure and extended the facility into the neighboring lot.

B. P. O. E. BUILDING.
OREGON CITY, OREGON

The residence of Maj. Thomas (left) and Sophia Charman (right), in 1888, prominently stood at 623 Main Street. In 1902, the new proprietor, Solomon Garde, relocated the dwelling to the adjacent lot and constructed "unquestionably, one of the finest buildings here," according to the *Oregon City Courier*. Jewelers and first tenants William Andresen, whose name remains over the central doorway, and Eliza Burmeister, purchased the structure by 1905. Well-known tenants included Howell & Jones Drug Store and Mr. Pix Photography Studio.

The 1840s Methodist Episcopal church building, initially located at Third Street, occupied 622 Main Street until 1890. That year, the growing congregation pulled the small structure back to face Seventh Street and constructed a larger Gothic-style edifice. An architectural modification in 1903, photographed the same year, raised the main building to accommodate commercial space below. After a fire consumed the structure in 1919, the congregation moved into the bluff-level Eastham house. Various retailers occupied the new 1920 single-story building over time.

Locals answered the patriotic call when the US government promoted the Third Liberty Loan Drive during World War I. Using donated materials and volunteer time, the residents erected a Liberty Loan Temple, photographed in 1918, on Seventh Street between Main Street and the elevator. The temple, decorated with strung lights and ornamental plants, provided a loan headquarters and drop-off center for humanitarian drives. After the war, the Women's Christian Temperance Union maintained the building until its demolition in 1919.

A new hydro-powered elevator, in 1915, offered access between Oregon City's levels—a favorable alternative to bluff-side staircases. Previously, noting the benefits of the new lift, the *Oregon Daily Journal* reported the "hill people" appeared as if "turkey trotting down Oregon City's gangplank" when descending the Seventh Street stairs. In 1955, a modern lift replaced the unreliable, electrically converted elevator. Photographed from Railroad Avenue, the old system remained in operation during construction. The train depot survived until the 1970s.

CHAPTER

2

BEYOND THE BEND
AND THE BRIDGE

The 1930s view south from the second story of the Frank Hopp building at 916 Main Street demonstrates a century of dramatic transformations. However, though the changed townscape is significant, recognizable architecture like the stately 1884 courthouse and the enduring Masonic Hall—landmarks that anchor this stretch of Main Street to the Seventh Street crossroads—preserve familiarity.

Andrina "Katie" Barclay dedicated her new building at 701 Main Street during a New Year's Eve celebration on January 1, 1895. Over time, Barclay's well-known tenants included druggist Linn Jones and attorney William Mulvey, who partnered as the building's proprietors in 1931. Architectural modifications before 1936 removed the crenelated parapets, followed by stucco layers that concealed the brick facade's classic details and Barclay's ornately scribed name. The landmark structure survives as one of lower Oregon City's last remaining 19th-century buildings.

William Singer's abandoned flouring mill, photographed in 1892, reportedly "a lodging house for tramps and a trysting place for not over-scrupulous lovers" (*Oregon City Courier*), was destroyed by fire in 1898. Adjacent were the Seventh Street steps, which had undergone periodic improvements due to weather and natural wear. The most significant, however, was in 1905, when an overhead bridge constructed to circumvent the tracks prompted the removal of the lower half of the stairs. The WPA reconstructed the entire staircase by 1939.

Dr. Forbes Barclay's 1849 home at 709 Main Street, photographed in 1890 with little Cis Pratt and her mother, Harriet, was one of Oregon City's earlier dwellings. The house was pushed back to Water Street by 1907 for the new Masonic Lodge and relocated again in 1937 to its present location at 719 Center Street. The Barclay House was added to the National Park System in 2003 and currently accommodates the McLoughlin Memorial Association and the National Park Service offices.

Beyond the Bend and the Bridge

Barclay's 1850s cherry tree, photographed about 1904, witnessed Main Street's growth as structures, like the 1884 fire hall (712 Main Street) and Gustave Friewald's c. 1905 building (714 Main Street), replaced lots and dwellings. The fire hall fell by 1925 to accommodate a new city hall building after the city's government decidedly remained on Main Street. Barclay's tree finally succumbed to modernization in 1907. Locals reported the loss of the "old friend" as "limb after limb . . . fell to the ground."

Shortly after local druggist Clyde Huntley constructed the 1892 single-story commercial building at 713 Main Street, he and his brother William established the Huntley Brothers Store, photographed in 1899. William managed retail goods, including books and stationery, and Clyde filled prescribed medications and tinctures. Harry Draper joined the brothers in 1922, and together, they founded the Huntley-Draper Drug Company. After a fire destroyed the building in 1986, the grounds, later paved, served as a parking lot.

Robert Caufield, later a county judge, came to Oregon with his family in 1847 and soon marketed "Groceries & Provisions" from his new general store at 723 Main Street. By the 1890s, the Caufields maximized their lot's utility and, like many, pulled their residence back to build multi-use structures. Photographed around 1897, Caufield's tenants included grocers, undertakers, a confectionery, and a photographer. A fire in the 1930s forced reconstruction, and the Caufields added shops within the space of the two buildings.

Clackamas County's decision to move the courthouse to the hill was not unprecedented. Indeed, the county's first courthouse, constructed in 1850, sat bluff-level on Madison Street between Sixth and Seventh. However, after a fire destroyed the two-story building in 1857, many—though not all—welcomed convening in nearby Main Street halls instead of the "out-of-the-way-place" on the bluff. Opposition aside, Main Street prevailed, and in 1884 the new courthouse, photographed in 1891 from the promenade was constructed.

BEYOND THE BEND AND THE BRIDGE

In 1895, brewer Henry Weinhard built the brick building at 802 Main Street, leasing to tenants like undertaker Roswell Holman and Bellomy & Busch Furnishings over time. Frank Busch occupied the building (photographed in 1900) until 1907, when the *Oregon City Enterprise* reported he "moved into his handsome new storeroom" at 1101–1107 Main Street. In 1920, the Weinhard Estate sold the building to the Hogg Brothers, tenants since 1913. The Busch family took ownership after the brothers retired in 1970.

Oregon City's early post office leased floor space from local merchants instead of operating from an independent facility. In 1913, this changed when the Weinhard estate acquired a five-year lease with the US government and, under contract, constructed a free-standing fireproof post office at 808 Main Street. Photographed in 1920, shortly after the contract's expiration, the post office, motivated by lower rent and ample carrier parking, had relocated to 506–508 Main Street. The Hogg Brothers replaced the small structure by 1925.

The Dr. John McLoughlin Institute, founded by Father Hillebrand in 1907, sat at 917 Main Street, near St. John's Catholic Church. Designed by Joseph Jacobberger, one of Portland's leading architects, the structure, photographed in 1935, accommodated up to 300 elementary and high school students. In 1948, St. John the Apostle Catholic School, an extension of the institute, opened on the hill at 516 Fifth Street. The old institute was then razed and replaced by a Safeway store and parking lot.

McLoughlin Institute.   OREGON CITY, Ore.

Druggist Elmer Charman (center), Lena (left), and their daughter June (right), photographed in 1887, occupied the elegant 1882 home at 902 Main Street until Elmer's death in 1905. By 1917, the house, converted into apartments, was relocated to the river's edge at Tenth and Water Streets, and the Miller-Parker Company constructed an automobile garage and showroom on the lot. After a fire in 1966 damaged the garage, new owners cleared the building's southwest corner walls for a parking lot.

BEYOND THE BEND AND THE BRIDGE

Freytag's Corner Grocery opened at 1320 Main Street in the 1880s after the family settled in Oregon City. Richard Freytag, standing in the doorway in 1895, enlarged the building around 1900 and, shortly after, sold the property to grocer Mary Harris, whose home remains adjacent at the rear. Mary's brother, Virginius Harris, renovated the building in 1912, adding second-floor apartments. The Harris family retained the property until 1945. Various grocers, restaurants, and taverns occupied the building over the decades.

Heavy downpours and melting snow between December 1922 and January 1923 brought substantial flooding into the region's low-lying areas. By January 3, the overflowing Willamette River overwhelmed Abernethy Creek and surged into lower Oregon City, forcing road and bridge closures. At the flood line between Thirteenth and Fourteenth Streets in 1923, observers on the Washington Street incline evaluated the rising waters that blocked access into Gladstone and threatened the Willamette Valley Southern Railway's trestle over Washington at Fifteenth Street.

BEYOND THE BEND AND THE BRIDGE

CHAPTER 3

ONTO THE HEIGHTS

In 1891, the *Oregon City Enterprise* announced improvements on upper Seventh Street, "where an ill-conditioned wagon road wound its tortuous way among the rocks and hills a city street is being built." Grading crews, photographed eight years later, in 1899, continued to work Seventh Street and simultaneously arterial streets as grading ordinances gradually passed—undertakings that continued into the 1920s.

Singer Hill Road, formerly a cliffside trail, connected wheeled traffic between Oregon City's lower and upper levels. However, despite occasional improvements, the road remained uneven, steep, and narrow. In 1895, when photographed, the *Oregon City* *Enterprise* reported that the road's exposed boulders required a "powerful grip on the seat and a steady nerve to keep from swearing while riding down and up the hill in a two-horse wagon." The city finally approved the road's partial paving in 1920.

Edward and Clara Eastham's home, once perched on the bluff's edge at 815 Center Street, was one of Oregon City's grand residences. Eastham, whose many achievements included producing hydro-powered electricity, died shortly after this 1891 photograph, just months after the home's completion. In 1920, after a fire gutted their Seventh and Main Street church, the Methodist Episcopal Church purchased and remodeled the Eastham dwelling to accommodate its congregation. The current structure replaced the converted house in 1950.

The Chase carriage house, constructed in 1892 at 610 High Street, first served as the family's temporary residence while they renovated their iconic bluff-side home. After James Chase died in 1910, his wife, Sarah, converted the upper level of their "nice stone barn" into living quarters. By the 1930s, the Heisleys, a married chiropractor team, purchased the building for their residence and practice. Though the Chase house met the wrecking ball in 1960, the carriage house, photographed in 1936, prevailed.

Agnes and Martin McDonough's home at 419 Fifth Street is one of the few structures in the McLoughlin neighborhood that retains Victorian Queen Anne elements. The dwelling, photographed in the 1960s, was one of two rentals built for saloon owner Martin McDonough of Brady & McDonough between 1896 and 1897. The McDonoughs lived in the home briefly before Martin sold his saloon interest to his partner Edward Brady and the couple relocated to Spokane, Washington.

By 1905, Walter Little and Charles Friedrich opened neighboring shops in Little's buildings at 512 and 514 Seventh Street. Photographed in 1908, Little (left) expanded his Main Street confectionery to the hill, and Friedrich (right), a blacksmith, established the only bluff-level hardware store. Friedrich moved to the Odd Fellows building at 602 Seventh Street in 1922, and Little subsequently updated the smaller structure. The current brick building was completed in 2016 after a fire in 2007 destroyed the historic structures.

ONTO THE HEIGHTS

Mary Elizabeth Stevens purchased the property at 602 Seventh Street in 1890. She resided in the home with her husband, Harley, photographed the same year, and their daughter Mertie until 1909, when they moved into their new residence directly behind. After the Independent Order of Odd Fellows (IOOF) purchased the property in 1921, they relocated the house to 923 Ninth Street, where it remains. Since 1922, the IOOF building has housed Friedrich's Hardware and a series of restaurants.

Mary Elizabeth and Harley Stevens Sr. hired architect Christopher Robbins in 1907 to design their new home at 603 Sixth Street. Robbins had recently completed Oregon City's Masonic Lodge and, in 1905, McMinnville's Hotel Elberton, known today as McMenamins' Hotel Oregon. Construction began in mid-1908, and the family took occupancy in 1909. Mary bequeathed the home, photographed in 1913, to her daughter Mertie, who, in turn, endowed the property to the Clackamas County Historical Society before she died in 1968.

Prominent attorney Joseph Hedges purchased the property at 603 John Adams Street in 1917, residing in the home until he and his wife, Lillian, passed in the 1940s. Afterward, the residence served as an all-female boardinghouse. The city claimed the structure in the 1950s for the Oregon City Police headquarters, photographed with police sergeants Robert Chester (left) and Stanley Orzechowski (right) in about 1960. The house was demolished in 1986 and replaced by the Francis Ermatinger House.

The city purchased the property at 620 Seventh Street in 1921 for the future city hall despite opposition favoring the Main Street location. Plans to relocate the fire station to upper Seventh Street met similar resistance. Opponents argued that removing the firehouse from the lower level left merchants vulnerable to devastating fires. Though the fire department, photographed in 1931, finally moved into the new building by 1925, City Hall's move to upper Seventh Street stalled until the 1940s.

Dr. John McLoughlin reserved the bluff side promenade and individual city blocks, including Seventh Street Park, photographed around 1890, for public use. The grounds, also known as City Park, accommodated community gatherings and maintained the local bandstand until 1912, when the city council designated the block for the Carnegie Library. The view over the daisy cover on John Adams Street gives the illusion of sparse inhabitation. However, the hundreds of pre-1900s homes remaining in this historic McLoughlin Conservation District prove otherwise.

Oregon City's First Congregational Church, familiarly known as Atkinson Memorial Church, was constructed at 710 Sixth Street in 1925 after a fire consumed their Main Street building. Photographed the same year, the new 20th-century Gothic-style structure, designed by Portland architect Willard Tobey, featured two asymmetrical towers and Povey Brothers stained-glass windows. Though the octagonal bell tower remains, the square tower, blamed for ongoing water leaks, was removed in 1958. However, the leaks persisted.

Capt. Ferdinand and Sarah Meldrum McCown's 1874 home at 415 Jefferson Street was initially constructed fronting Fifth Street, though later turned. McCown was an Oregon City attorney and served three consecutive terms as city mayor. Sarah actively advocated for equal rights and, in 1894, was appointed vice president of the Oregon State Women Suffrage Association for Clackamas County. The house, a rental when photographed in 1898 with unidentified tenants, is one of Oregon City's last remaining examples of Colonial Revival architecture.

Around 1918, Dr. Edward McLean encouraged Ida Hutchinson, a dressmaker, to open a maternity hospital in her home at 1104 Sixth Street. Photographed in the 1930s, the facility evolved into Hutchinson General Hospital, one of two operating hospitals in Oregon City. The organization's physicians converted the hospital into a not-for-profit and, in 1954, established the Doctors' Hospital. The facility relocated to Division Street in the 1960s and was later renamed Providence Willamette Falls Medical Center.

ONTO THE HEIGHTS

Duane and George Ely established the Ely Brothers firm in 1889. Initially, the brothers operated in Elyville, an upper Oregon City neighborhood, but later relocated to 906 Seventh Street. In February 1903, during the construction of their new implements warehouse, George sold his interest to Ed Carter, who, by May, sold to the grocery firm Horton & Jack. Duane Ely (right), photographed in 1903 with an unidentified associate, retained the building until the 1950s. The structure stood along Seventh Street until the mid-1970s.

Adventurers Gilbert Church, photographed at his residence in 1891, and his wife, Mindwell, summited Mt. Hood several times—their daughter Hattie was reportedly the youngest to do so at nine. In 1891, shortly after Gilbert completed the double dwelling, the *Enterprise* newspaper reported that the "harmonious" paint tones gave the residence at 914 Seventh Street an "elegant appearance." After 1910, the Churches moved to Gladstone, and the structure served as various boardinghouses, the Seventh Street Hotel, a restaurant, and apartments.

ONTO THE HEIGHTS

Anticipating upcoming street improvements, in 1891, the *Enterprise* announced, "With the new grade to be established on Seventh Street, and improved sidewalks, it will become one of the handsomest streets in Oregon City." Six years later, Seventh Street, photographed in 1897 near Jackson, remained under development. With a notable bluff-level population, pedestrians welcomed plank sidewalks instead of dirt or muddy paths. Though solid surfaces secured a footing, several decades passed before trees offered shade along the uphill trek.

The Seventh Street School, at 1404 Seventh Street, was designated the Eastham School a year after its 1893 construction, posthumously recognizing Ed Eastham, one of Oregon City's leading citizens. Serving upper Oregon City's increasing population, a new structural addition, constructed just before this 1909 photograph, nearly doubled the building's size. The current brick structure replaced the bell-towered school in 1950 and educated elementary-age students until 1992. Until recently, the facility served as the Eastham Community Center.

Today, the concrete stairs and stone retaining wall at 1403 Seventh Street appear to be surviving remnants from the church property removed around 2010. However, the stairs and walls had bordered Seventh Street since 1890, when county judge and state senator Gordon E. Hayes inhabited what the *Oregon Courier* later called his "elegantly furnished cottage." By 1912, the Amrines, whose daughters graced the grounds the following year, acquired the home. The Amrines, and their heirs, owned the property until 1933.

Real estate agent Ernest Elliot and his wife Lillie resided in the c. 1890s home at 426 Division Street from 1901 until their deaths in the early 1940s. Initially a single-story dwelling, the structure was raised around 1902 to accommodate a new main level below, benefitting the family's seven children—the two youngest, Ruth (center) and Raymond (right), photographed with Lillie in 1910. The residence retains its original character, despite the removal of minor scrollwork and the petite roofwalk.

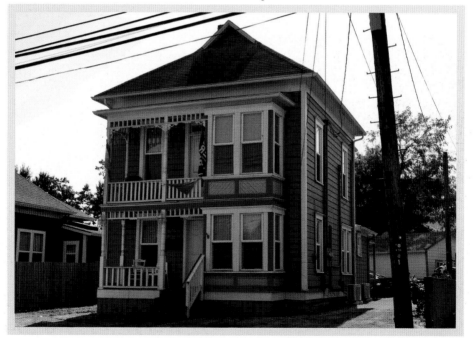

ONTO THE HEIGHTS

Oregon City's first free-standing high school opened in 1911 at 1110 John Q. Adams Street. The campus, photographed in 1918, featured a singular classic brick structure until the addition of a gymnasium in 1921. An increased student population encouraged the construction of a larger high school in 1936, and the old building functioned as a junior high. Today, a parking lot serves the surrounding facilities, and only the gymnasium and concrete steps on Eleventh and Twelfth Streets remain.

The 1889 Twelfth Street School was renamed Barclay School in 1894 as a monument to education advocate Dr. Forbes Barclay. The grand structure replaced the worn 1850 Clackamas County Female Seminary building, which had since functioned as Oregon City's first long-running public school. Photographed in 1909 near 817 Twelfth Street, the Barclay School served until its 1935 demolition. A WPA grant aided the construction of the current Barclay School in 1936. Though the classrooms closed in 1985, the school district maintains the facility.

James and Sarah Roake's house at 720 Eleventh Street was originally a single-story structure. However, shortly before Sarah and their son Verne posed for this 1895 photograph, Roake hired builder Jack Jones, who moved the one-story residence back, raised the old house to add a new main floor, and attached a "modern in style" two-story addition. Roake's community prominence rose when he established the Oregon City Iron Works, which ran for three generations. The home remains a private residence.

In September 1911, two nurses and their colleague relocated their flourishing Wildwood Hospital from an upper hill in Oregon City to a larger home on Washington Street near Tenth, previously owned by attorney Carey Johnson. By 1918, after continued success, the house, photographed around 1913, was cleared, and the site evolved substantially, extending to Washington and Eleventh Street. The hospital shuttered around 1976, and a care facility, now closed since 2020, opened in its place.

The 1847 residence of William and Louisa Holmes, at the Rose Farm, is one of Oregon's oldest surviving buildings. Holmes, Clackamas County's first sheriff under the Oregon Territory, famously hosted Joseph Lane's inauguration as Oregon's first territorial governor in 1849. Photographed in 1900, Holmes' daughters, Minnie (top left) and Molly (top right), hosted John Meldrum (top center) and (bottom left-right) Mary and David Thompson and Georgina Meldrum. The McLoughlin Memorial Association preserves the Holmes House Museum at 536 Holmes Lane.

The 1851 Ainsworth House, previously Mount Pleasant, was constructed on Oregon City's rural edge for Capt. John Ainsworth and his wife, Jane. Ainsworth arrived in Oregon in 1850 to captain the new steamboat *Lot Whitcomb*. He later founded the Oregon Steam Navigation Company and, by 1859, moved with his family to Portland. The Greek Revival-style home, photographed in 1934, retained its remote surroundings until the 1990s. The preserved home and gardens, now an event venue, are located at 19130 Lot Whitcomb Drive.

CHAPTER

ROADS, RIVER, AND RAIL

In the 1920s, the tired suspension bridge linking Oregon City and West Linn could no longer sustain the continuously increasing motor traffic that crossed the Willamette River along the Pacific Highway. The replacement, the new Arch Bridge, utilized the old suspension supports as scaffolding to circumvent regular water traffic, such as the sternwheeler *Claire*, photographed in 1922.

69

Art Heath purchased the 1926 service station and barbeque at 201 S. Second Street in 1944. Shortly after, Heath (right), photographed in the 1940s with an unidentified associate, operated Art's Cafe, a well-known diner. Though Heath sold the business by 1960, the name and homestyle cooking remained. In 2001, road adjustments at Second Street and US Route 99E limited diner parking, and the cafe closed despite subsequent attempts to reopen. In 2006, new owners converted the landmark into a pub.

ROADS, RIVER, AND RAIL

The Willamette Falls Locks opened to river traffic on January 1, 1873, linking the upper and lower stretches of the Willamette River. Prior, hired transportation portaged goods and passengers between Oregon City and Canemah. Though the new locks advantaged river transportation, without the stop, Canemah's prominence waned. The south view from the suspension bridge in 1888 revealed the raw basalt that provided a natural foundation for the superhighway in the 1930s. (Past, courtesy Old Oregon Photos and WFLHAC.)

In the 1920s, automobile traffic along the Pacific Highway, a travel artery between British Columbia and the US-Mexico border, passed over the new Arch Bridge and through downtown Oregon City. However, Water Street remained undeveloped, leaving only one lateral improved road—Main Street—to serve the route through the lower business district. In the 1930s, the new superhighway, (McLoughlin Boulevard), photographed in 1937 from the bluff at Fifth Street, converted Water Street into a main thoroughfare, circumventing the city's core.

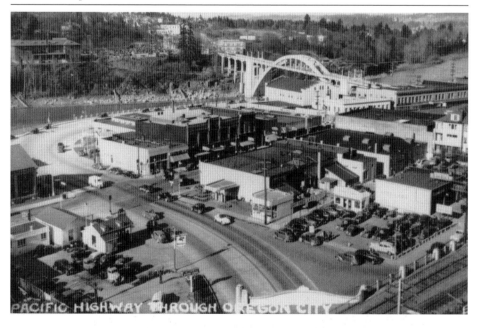

ROADS, RIVER, AND RAIL

Conductor Mack Howell (lower left), with unidentified crew and passengers, stopped at 512 Main Street in 1893, shortly after the completion of the new electric railway, which shuttled passengers between Oregon City and Portland. However, by 1915, jitney buses and automobiles, able to reach outlying communities, rivaled street cars, and the popularity of track-bound transportation decreased. Nevertheless, like times past, Oregon City's Main Street remains a primary route for public transportation.

The new Pacific Greyhound Lines Bus Depot at 214 Sixth Street, photographed shortly after completion in 1949, replaced the previous depot, once a jitney stop, on lower Seventh Street near the elevator. The new depot accommodated motorcoach traffic routed through Oregon City, a stop along a transcontinental network of commercial bus routes. Overnight passengers found accommodations at the adjacent Terminal Hotel and hot meals in nearby restaurants. The depot operated through the 1950s and has since housed various businesses.

ROADS, RIVER, AND RAIL

Harvey Jackson's Bicycle Shop stood at 714 Main Street—716 Main Street today. A machinist by trade, Jackson could "mend or repair anything from a bicycle to a steam engine." The *Oregon City Courier*'s praise arose from Jackson's self-made steam-powered automobile, pictured after its completion in 1902. Jackson relocated to Portland the same year, and a confectionery and later a jeweler occupied the space. The row of wood-clad structures gradually fell in favor of fire-resistant brick buildings.

The Roos building at 722–724 Main Street opened in 1914, providing second-floor rooms to the Commercial Club. The organization, photographed with the Automobile Club shortly after the building's completion, remained until 1919, when they returned to their rooms in the Masonic hall. Over time, the multi-roomed building maintained various tenants, including a barber shop, real estate brokers, saloons, and merchants. In the background, the *Oregon City Courier* building at Eighth Street and Railroad Avenue stands in the early stages of construction.

During Oregon's dry summer months, when city funding permitted, contracted drivers like Clarence Heskett, photographed in 1915 at 720 Main Street, operated the sprinkler wagon to control road dust from the unpaved streets. Generally routed along Molalla Avenue and Main, Seventh, Fifth, and Center Streets, the wagon's spray, usually water or oil, dampened the road. However, residents on less traveled streets had to hire the service privately. In the background, the temporary 1913 post office stands neighboring the Weinhard Building.

One of Oregon City's central steamboat docks sat adjacent to the Clackamas County Courthouse down Eighth Street's steep and rocky slope. Capt. John Graham and his Oregon City Transportation Company leased the Eighth Street dock where their fleet, including the *Altona* photographed in 1890, operated passenger and freight service along the Willamette River. However, steamboat use dwindled by the 1920s, and US Route 99E's construction the following decade leveled the dock, though a side staircase remains for river access.

At the turn of the 20th century, communities, notably those joined by the electric railway, underwent periods of architectural development. Increased lumber demand prompted the emergence of rural and municipal sawmills, each vying for regional or interstate contracts. The unidentified teamsters from Colton's mill, photographed in 1906, paused alongside the Knapp building at Tenth and Main Streets after steering their contracted load down Singer Hill Road. The brick structure, built in 1904 at 922 Main Street, stood until the 1930s.

Before improvements, Singer Hill Road's steep descent and blind turn at the base while simultaneously intersecting with an active railroad crossing was ruthless against failed brakes and startled wagon teams. In 1907, shortly after the *Enterprise-Courier* referenced the hazardous intersection as "Deadman's Crossing," the Southern Pacific Railroad stationed a flagman, photographed in 1917—though unidentified—at the Tenth Street junction. Today, flashing lights at Singer Hill's crest and electronic crossing gates at the base signal for passing trains.

ROADS, RIVER, AND RAIL

In 1923, a raging fire decimated the 1890 Congregational Church at 1024 Main Street. The congregation relocated to Sixth and John Adams Streets on the hill, and the Boguslaskis and Engebrechts constructed a new auto garage and showroom on the lot in the same year. Logan Chevrolet moved into the facility in 1928 but vacated soon after this 1933 photograph. Various dealerships and motor companies occupied the building until around 1987, when the building was converted to serve the county.

The Pacific Highway Garage, one of many auto-centered businesses in the city, marketed Ford and Studebaker automobiles and offered cars for hire. The garage moved into Busch's new building at 1117 Main Street in 1913, photographed with manager Morton Park the same year. After a fire in 1922 destroyed their neighboring structure, Busch Furnishings moved to this location. The building was demolished in the 1970s after Tom Busch Home Furnishings returned the family business to the Weinhard Building.

CHAPTER 4

A SENSE OF COMMUNITY

During the early 20th century, Oregon City's celebratory events were spectacular. Though festivities often featured firework displays, acrobats, live music, and street dancing, they all included various competitive events planned around the city. From three-legged races to steamboat races, photographed during the 1937 Territorial Days celebration, the festival-going population guaranteed lively attendance and community support.

In 1887, Oregon became the first state to pass legislation recognizing Labor Day. However, regardless of state and nationwide celebrations, Oregon City did not organize its first large-scale Labor Day event until 1902. The long-awaited festival featured hundreds of parade participants representing regional labor unions, civic organizations, and fraternal societies. The northbound parade, photographed in 1902 at Fifth and Main Streets, eventually proceeded south toward Canemah Park, where festivities continued. The holiday celebration closed with a grand display of fireworks.

A SENSE OF COMMUNITY

The Second Oregon Volunteer Infantry accepted President McKinley's call in April 1898, requesting military aid during the Spanish–American War. By early May, approximately sixty young Oregon City men, representing Company I, marched to an awaiting train at Seventh Street and Railroad Avenue. After reaching San Francisco, a steamer transported the soldiers to Manila, Philippines. The corner bank and the single-story building at 215 Seventh Street, initially the Pacific Highway Garage, replaced these wood-sided structures in the 1920s.

Like today, 19th-century firefighters joined in celebratory parades. However, their participation extended to post-parade hose cart races that divided volunteer fire companies, though united as first responders, into competitive opponents. Photographed marching north on Main and Seventh during the 1893 Fourth of July parade, Oregon City's Hook and Ladder Company, with canine mascots in tow, prepared for upcoming races. The following year, Katie Barclay moved the house, decorated with bunting, back to Water Street for her new brick building.

A SENSE OF COMMUNITY

William Long capitalized on the popularity of vaudeville and moving pictures when he opened the Star Theater at 720 Main Street in 1912. Though Long (center), photographed in 1913, primarily featured motion pictures and hosted touring stage performers, he additionally provided a gathering venue for schools and organizations. However, like the Liberty Theatre, also one of Long's enterprises, attendance dwindled in the 1950s. After closing its doors to screen and stage entertainment, the venue housed various public houses.

The highly anticipated Territorial Days festivities brought statewide, often historically dressed, celebrants into Oregon City. Costumed men, typically bearded, sported large black hats, neckerchiefs, and plaid shirts, while women modeled heirloom or reproduction attire. Events like the Territorial Days Women's Parade, observed from Eighth and Main Street during the 1936 celebration, presented opportunities to show off vintage costumes. Later, crowds gathered at Library Park for the historical dress competition where women's costumes, ranked by period, were judged for authenticity.

A SENSE OF COMMUNITY

William Long's Liberty Theatre, photographed in 1926, opened at 815 Main Street in 1921. The popular venue provided local entertainment until it closed in the 1960s. After installing a false ceiling to conceal the theater's higher reaches, retailers and offices occupied the main floor. Years of deterioration led to its demolition in 2004, despite appeals from preservationists. The Liberty Plaza, a hub for local festivals and events, now occupies the site. (Past, courtesy Old Oregon Photos and WFLHAC.)

2nd Annual Territorial Days Kick-Off Breakfast, Oregon City. July 8 1936

The parish hall at 102 Ninth Street, constructed in 1930, annexed the neighboring St. Paul's Episcopal Church and rectory. The hall furnished a venue for social gatherings, including the photographed Territorial Days Kick-off Breakfast in 1936. However, by 1945, the congregation had relocated to Ninth and Washington Streets, and a parking lot and bank replaced the older buildings. Though various organizations occupied the structure over the decades, new owners converted the nearly 100-year-old parish hall into a brewpub in 1995.

A SENSE OF COMMUNITY

The American Brass Band Movement inspired the formation of amateur bands nationwide in communities like Oregon City, bringing lively music to local celebrations. The city's brass band, photographed looking south on Main Street at Ninth in 1900, stands before the Elmer Charman house (left) and Julius Logus house (right). The homes characterize the finer residences that once lined Main Street. Though the Charman house moved in 1917, the Logus house remained at the corner until its demolition in the 1950s.

After Hawley Pulp and Paper Mill purchased Dr. John McLoughlin's 1845–1846 house and property in 1908, the new McLoughlin Memorial Association arranged for the home's relocation to the bluff-side park. However, the move met resistance. Opponents insisted the building's poor condition would decrease property values, and by 1909 the *Oregon City Enterprise* reported 202 petitioners filed to vote against "placing old buildings on the park block." Finally, despite ongoing opposition, the McLoughlin House, newly renovated, was dedicated on September 5, 1909.

A SENSE OF COMMUNITY

The third annual Territorial Days celebration in 1937 was well-attended by locals and visitors alike. The festival's opening day parade, the route lined with spectators, marched down Seventh Street to High Street's perpendicular approach. The procession, photographed as it bypassed the Singer Hill turnoff, paraded to 99E, then continued north down Main Street toward Kelley Field—the parade's terminus at the foot of Washington. Salem's *Capital Journal* reported an estimated 22,000 people had attended the celebration's closing ceremonies.

Oregon City's first Territorial Days, celebrated in 1935, opened two years after Prohibition had ended. Until then, laws banned merchants, like Oregon City Cold Storage, from publicly advertising alcoholic beverages. Resting on the wagon's tailgate around 1936, civic member Frank Perrine (bottom) and unidentified wagon guides lingered at Jackson and Seventh Streets before joining the Territorial Days procession. In the background, Maynard McGeehan's house (left) and Alison Pease's (right) have stood guard over Seventh Street for over a century.

Oregon City's first municipal swimming pool, primarily WPA-funded, opened in 1935 at Eleventh and Madison Streets. However, the popular summer hangout, photographed around 1955, lacked a filtration system and continuously required additional measures to mitigate health risks. The pool finally closed in 1965, and Latourette Park opened in its place. In 2015, Girl Scout Troop 45064, "Latourette's Army," partnered with Metro and local supporters to advocate for the park's revitalization and universal accessibility. After years of dedicated work, the new park opened in 2021.

DISCOVER THOUSANDS OF LOCAL HISTORY BOOKS FEATURING MILLIONS OF VINTAGE IMAGES

Arcadia Publishing, the leading local history publisher in the United States, is committed to making history accessible and meaningful through publishing books that celebrate and preserve the heritage of America's people and places.

Find more books like this at
www.arcadiapublishing.com

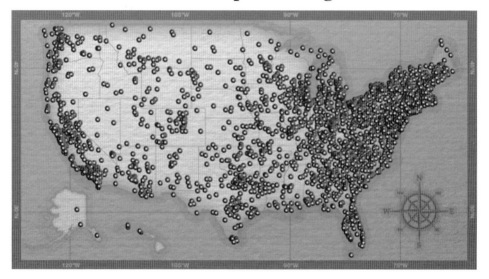

Search for your hometown history, your old stomping grounds, and even your favorite sports team.